Activ

Dorothy Hunt

JAN MORROW

All Year Round

Longman

LONGMAN GROUP UK LIMITED

Longman House
Burnt Mill, Harlow, Essex CM20 2JE, England
and Associated Companies throughout the world

© Jan Morrow 1988

All rights reserved. No part of this publication
may be reproduced, stored in a retrieval system,
or transmitted in any form or by any means, electronic,
mechanical, photocopying, recording or otherwise ,
without the prior written permission of the copyrigh owner.

First published 1988
Third impression 1989

British Library Cataloguing in Publication Data

Morrow, Jan, 1952—
    Activities all year round.
    1. Seasonal activities for children — For
    children
    I. Title   II. Series
    790.1'922

    ISBN 0-582-01764-5

Set in Linotype 11/12pt Frutiger 45 Light

Produced by Longman Group (FE) Ltd
Printed in Hong Kong

Contents

Christmas

Nativity costumes   7
The nativity play   9
A time for giving   9
An alternative Christmas tree   10
A garland of Christmas stockings   10
Visiting the Christmas lights   11
Christmas card jigsaws   11
Paper doily snowflakes   11
Simple experiments with ice   12
Jack Frost windows   12
A frosty collage   13
Marshmallow mince pies   13
Winter bird cake   14
A snowman   14
A cracker of home-made bath salts   15
A snow storm   16
An angel   16
A stained-glass window Christmas card   17

Valentine's Day

Fruit painting   18
Design some family stamps   18
My favourite things   18
The take-a-letter game   19
Who are you going to marry?   19
Bread flowers for a Valentine posy   20
Dream cups   20
Love heart earrings   21
A pressed-flower posy   21
Pink dream mousse   22
A Valentine card   22

Mother's Day

Make-up sessions and dressing up   23
A bracelet   23
Chocolate fruit   23
An orange peel necklace   24
A flower salad   24
Perfumed pictures   25
A sweet smeller   25
A daffodil Mother's Day card   26
A little ballerina   26
A mother's day picture poem   27
Washing the car   27

Easter

An Easter egg treasure hunt   28
Decorating eggs   28
An Easter mobile   28
A decorated Easter cake   29
A patch of garden   29
Growing seeds, pips and stones   30
Grow a picture   31
A flower petal poem   32
Easter bonnets   32
An Easter rabbit card   33
Egg shell heads   33
Marzipan animals   34
A spring flower posy   34

Father's Day

Father's whiskers picture poem   35
Soap carving   35
A piggy bank   35
An express train tea   36
Cheese rockets   36
A pen tidy for dad's desk   37
A Father's Day card   37

Halloween

Shadow Puppets   38
Tail on the cat   38
Abracadabra   39
A witch's hat   39
The cauldron game   40
Black spells   40
Hunting the ghost   40
The witch's nose   41
Ice-cream witches   41
A witches brew   42
Witch's fingers   42
A spider   43
A paper witch   43
Edible nasties   44
A Halloween scratch picture   44

Bonfire night

Make an un-guy   45
The guy race game   45
A bonfire night safety poster   45
A torn paper bonfire collage   45
A rocket bottle   46
A bonfire picture poem   46
Bonfire masks   47
Catherine wheels   47
Chocolate leaves   48
Potato bake   48
Smoke pictures   49
A rocket on a stick   49

Birthdays

Party themes   50
Butter cream frosting   50

A jumble party theme   50
A jumble party invitation   51
A jumble party cake   51
Jumble party games   51

An animal party theme   53
An animal party invitation   53
An animal party cake   53
Animal party games   53

A cowboys and Indians party theme   54
A cowboys and Indians party invitation   55
A cowboys and Indians party cake   55
Cowboys and Indians party games   55

A pirates party theme   56
A pirate party invitation   56
A pirate party cake   57
Pirate party games   57

A fairy party theme   58
A fairy party invitation   58
A fairy party cake   58
Fairy party games   58

A newspaper party theme   59
A newspaper party invitation   59
A newspaper party cake   60
Newspaper party games   60

Birthday surprises   62
Kitten cakes   63
An edible zoo   64
Biscuit faces   62
Popcorn   62
Individual candle cakes   63
A birthday balloon card   64
A birthday badge   64

Introduction

This book is for inquisitive, interested, fun-loving children between the ages of 7 and 13 (who sometimes get bored) and for their parents who like to share the excitement and fun of growing up with them.

It is based on the cycle of festivals and celebrations which make up the year and contains ideas and advice for getting the most out of the time that the family shares together, as well as sources of further information in many areas. The activities described are easy to follow and encourage children to develop a sense of independence and confidence in their own abilities; at the same time they heighten their awareness of important events in the family calendar. These learning and fun activities which children can carry out on their own or with their parents are not only valuable in themselves, they also extend the enjoyment of traditional family celebrations.

Activities and Learning

In this book there are ideas for activities for children between the ages of 7 and 13. The areas covered focus on the family festivities and celebrations that parents and children share during the course of the year. Each area contains a wide range of related activities which involve the child in:

- reading practice
- simple scientific experiments
- creative writing
- nature study

In addition, at the end of every section there is a selection of cooking and model making activities which involve the child in simple mathematics as well as creativity.

Activities and Fun

The activities described in this book are designed to be educational, but, just as importantly, they are designed to be fun. They help with those "I'm bored" moments that every parent knows by involving children in interesting and exciting things to do. At the same time, they provide enjoyment through the feelings of achievement that come from the completion of an activity. If the activity is one shared with the parents, this itself is a source of pleasure and satisfaction for children; if it is one which the child has worked out for himself, it provides an enjoyable boost to his self-confidence. The element of fun and enjoyment in all the activities in the book is paramount.

None of the activities in this book requires complicated equipment or aparatus; they all use everyday objects found around the home. Whenever possible, writing or models made by children should be displayed attractively so that they can share their sense of achievement with the rest of the family. Ideally there should also be a table top for the display of three-dimensional objects and a wall where mounted writing and paintings can be arranged.

You and Your Child

The activities in this book aim to entertain your child and also, within a framework of fun, to develop her basic skills, to provide opportunities for creativity, and to increase her general knowledge of the environment. Festivals and celebrations provide a focus for you and your child to share together the excitement and the fun of growing up.

christmas

Nativity costumes

It isn't necessary to spend hours slaving over a sewing machine to produce effective nativity costumes. The following costumes are quick to make and the fabric for costume making doesn't need to be expensive. Most of the items can be found around the home or, failing that, jumble sales will provide beautiful material for only a few pence.

A robe for the angel

For younger children an old white pillowcase with holes cut out for the head and arms is most suitable.

For larger children, cut a rectangle, 150cm by 45cm, from an old white sheet and make a hole large enough for the child's head in the centre of the rectangle. Cut out a thin strip of white material to form a belt.

An angel halo

Use a strip of white card, 3cm by 55cm, with a band of silver tinsel attached along its length. Measure the child's head and sellotape the strip accordingly.

Alternatively just make a headband from silver tinsel.

Angel wings

These are notoriously difficult to make realistically, but a very simple wing substitute can be made by creating a tinsel strip wristband. Cut a piece of wide, white elasticated tape to the correct size for the child's wrist and sew the tape together to form a band. Sew strips of tinsel and white ribbon to the outside of the wristband. When the angel has her arms outstretched the tinsel and ribbon can look very pretty. Alternatively, white net curtains can be pinned into position on the back of the angel's robe and the loose material attached to wristbands.

All this certainly makes children LOOK angelic. No guarantees about anything else!

A king's crown

Take a strip of card, 55cm by 12cm. Decorate the card with shiny paper cut into diamond shapes, glitter and tinsel. Cut a pattern along one edge. Check the size of the child's head and sellotape the crown accordingly.

A king's cloak

Find a rectangular piece of material – the exact measurement rather depends on the size of your child. Remember, the richer the colour the more king-like it will look and curtain material is preferable as it is often a heavier quality.

Fold over a 10cm strip along one of the longer edges of the rectangle and sew this into position. Thread a long piece of ribbon or tape through the centre of the strip and then pull the material together until you have a gathered cloak.

The shepherds or Joseph

For this costume you will need:

- two old ties
- one of dad's old shirts (preferably striped)
- a rectangular piece of material

The shirt doesn't need to be cut to size. If the sleeves are too long they can easily be rolled up. Use one of the ties around the child's waist and the other tie fastened around the child's head (like a browband) to keep the rectangle of material in position.

Mary

By tradition Mary wears blue. If you haven't any blue material, it might be possible to dye an old sheet with a blue fabric dye. Cold water dyes are available from most chemists.

Mary's dress can be made in the same way as the angel's robe, i.e. use a rectangle of fabric with a round hole cut in the centre. Mary's head-dress can be made from a rectangle of the same material. The belt for around her waist and the headband could be made from strips of white ribbon.

The donkey

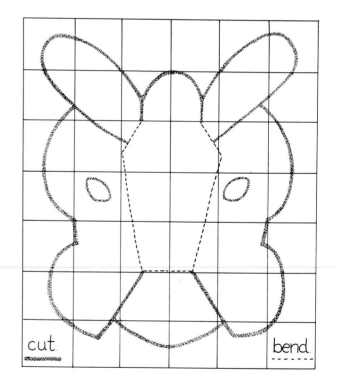

cut.

bend.

Using the illustration as a guide, draw the outline shape of the donkey's head on to some card. Cut round the outline and along the dotted lines and fold the card accordingly.

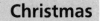

The nativity play

When provided with a dressing-up box of nativity costumes, your children and their friends will undoubtedly have their own ideas on the production of a nativity play. Children adore putting on surprise plays for adults to watch.

A simple suggestion that you might make, however, is that the dialogue or speaking parts could be replaced with mime and that the whole play could be performed to a tape of suitably beautiful music. Such a play needs far less in the way of preparation or rehearsal and even very young brothers and sisters can join in.

A time for giving

Often the true spirit of Christmas is overlooked by children. They can be so excited by the thought of their own expected presents that they forget that there is just as much, if not more, pleasure to be gained from the act of giving.

Encourage your child to make his or her own presents for friends or relatives. Not only is this less expensive but the personal touch is always appreciated. There are numerous ideas within this book which would make superb presents.

As well as making presents for friends and relatives, your child could also make a present for an elderly neighbour or even make a batch of sweets for an old people's home.

The way presents are wrapped and presented is just as important as the present itself. Personalised wrapping paper is fun to make. Wall lining paper or brown wrapping paper is probably the least expensive paper you can buy and this can be decorated either by printing shapes on to the paper with a cut potato and paint, or by drawing suitable pictures on to the paper with felt-tip pens.

A basket for home-made sweets

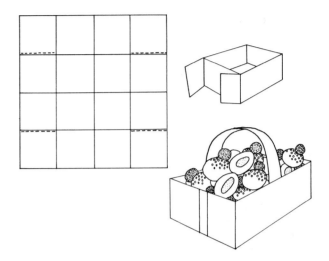

Take a square of thin card, 15cm by 15cm. Fold the card in half four times so that when it is opened out you have 16 squares. On each of the four corners slit the corner squares to the first crease. These corner squares are then folded over and glued on to the two end centre squares. This forms a square, box-shaped basket. Attach a strip of card across the centre of the box to create a handle.

The basket can be decorated in a variety of ways – with glitter, or ribbon, or cut-out Christmas motifs from last year's Christmas cards. Alternatively, sweets can be wrapped in coloured cellophane and tied with a pretty ribbon.

Children might also be encouraged to give some of their good quality but rarely used toys to one of the local charities collecting and distributing toys at Christmas. Or perhaps, with a grown-up's help, they could organise some neighbourhood carol singing and give the proceeds to a charity.

An alternative Christmas tree

Take a winter walk through some local woodland and together with your child find a suitably sized fallen branch. The exact size rather depends on where you intend to put it in the house. The branch should be as full of twigs as possible.

On your return home allow the branch to dry out and then ask the children to paint the branch with white emulsion paint. When the branch has dried, stand it in a pot of earth and decorate it.

The homemade decorations could include:

- clean milk bottle tops
- ribbons
- strings of peanuts in their shells (perhaps sprayed silver)
- wrapped sweets
- egg box bells (cut out the egg cups from egg boxes and sprinkle with glue and glitter)
- yogurt pot bells (cover empty yogurt pots with tinfoil)
- loo roll chimes (cover empty toilet roll tubes with tinfoil and wrap a piece of tinsel around the middle of each one)
- fir cones (these could also be sprayed silver)
- cotton wool for a snowy effect
- glitter could be stuck directly on to the branches with a little glue

Christmas branches can look extremely attractive and of course they are much less expensive than the traditional shop-bought Christmas tree.

A garland of Christmas stockings

Help your child to take some white paper and draw and cut out as many simple stocking shapes as possible. Each stocking needs to be about 20cm long. It might be easier if you make a template of a stocking shape out of thick card and draw round this.

Decorate the stockings. Paint some, and cut out pictures of toys from some old catalogues and stick these on to the rest.

Decide where you want to hang the stockings. Put some string or ribbon in position and fasten the stockings to it with some paper clips.

Visiting the Christmas lights

Wait until dark, dress up warmly and then take the family on a trip into the local town to look at the lights. Most towns put up illuminated street decorations at Christmas time and the shops themselves look extremely pretty with their Christmas decorations in the windows.

And when you get home, make it a special evening by having some favourite warming soup and crusty French bread.

Christmas card jigsaws

When Christmas is over, your child can use the old Christmas cards to make jigsaws.

Spread some glue inside each card and then place them underneath a heavy weight so that they will dry flat. When the glue has dried, cut the cards into pieces. Obviously the younger the child the fewer the pieces.

Help your child to put the pictures back together again and when he has finished, pop the card jigsaws into envelopes to keep safe until next time.

Winter provides a marvellous opportunity for your child to observe the effects of low temperatures on water and other natural objects. The following five activities provide further exploration and creative expression within a wintery theme.

Paper doily snowflakes

Ask your child to place a paper doily on top of a sheet of coloured paper and use a brush to carefully dab white paint over all the tiny holes in the doily.

When all the holes have been covered with paint, peel the doily away from the paper. Underneath you will see a pretty snowflake pattern. A very impressive picture can be made by cutting out lots of these snowflakes, dabbing them with glue and silver glitter, and arranging them on a sheet of coloured paper. Alternatively, stick them on to windows, or hang them in groups to make a mobile.

Simple experiments with ice

Two simple experiments to show the child how water expands when frozen can be made by collecting together:

- an empty plastic margarine or ice-cream tub with lid
- three pencils
- a strip of adhesive plaster

Experiment number one

Fill the margarine tub up to the brim with water. Carefully press the lid down on the tub, and place the tub in a frozen food compartment. After several hours your child should be able to see that the lid has been pushed off the tub by the ice.

Experiment number two

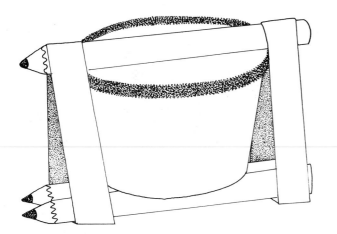

This experiment demonstrates just how powerful the force generated by expanding ice is. Fill the tub to the top with water and press down the lid. Lay one pencil across the top of the tub and two pencils side by side across the bottom of the tub.

Stretch the adhesive plaster around the ends of both the top and bottom pencils to hold the lid firmly in place.

Place the tub in a frozen food compartment and wait a few hours. Your child will find that the force of the expanding ice has been sufficient to break the top pencil in half as the lid was pushed from the tub.

Jack Frost windows

Collect together:

- a mixing bowl
- a sponge
- a cup
- a spoon
- washing soda (bath salts or Epsom Salts would also work)
- hot water

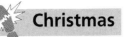

Help your child to put a cup of washing soda in the bowl. Add a cup of hot water and stir with the spoon until the crystals disappear.

Dip the sponge into the warm liquid and wipe it over the surface of a window. After about twenty minutes the liquid dries leaving behind frost-like crystals. These can easily be removed with a damp cloth.

Marshmallow mince pies

Collect together:

- 125g of ready made shortcrust pastry
- a jar of mincemeat
- 12 pink and white marshmallows
- 3 glace cherries cut into quarters
- a rolling pin
- a flour sifter
- a patty tin with a dozen sections
- a round pastry cutter
- a teaspoon
- a wire cooling rack

To make the tarts

1 Roll out the pastry on a floured surface. Cut out twelve circles of pastry and use these to line the patty tins.
2 Spoon a little mincemeat into each pastry case and bake in a preheated hot oven, (200C, Gas mark 6) for 10 to 15 minutes.
3 When the tarts are ready, remove them from the oven and place a marshmallow in the centre of each one. Return the tarts to the oven for 1 minute or just long enough to melt the marshmallow slightly.
4 Take the tarts out of the oven and carefully place a piece of cherry on top of each tart. Place them on a wire rack to cool.

A frosty collage

Make a collection of as many different shiny, silver items as possible, for example, silver toffee paper, tinsel, silver glitter, tinfoil, milk bottle tops and dried peas and other beans which have been sprayed silver.

Suggest your child glues the shiny, silver objects on to a dark piece of paper. It really isn't necessary to create a "picture" of something as the quality of shininess is enough on its own.

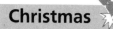

Winter bird cake

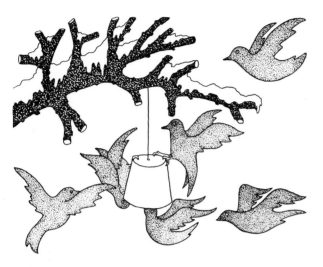

Collect together:

- 2 empty yogurt pots
- 2 pieces of string about 45cm long
- scissors
- 125g lard
- a saucepan
- a large bowl
- a dessertspoon
- a selection of the following: breadcrumbs, chopped bacon rind, chopped apple, currants, cake or biscuit crumbs, peanuts

To make the bird cake

1 Make a large knot on the end of each piece of string. Make a small hole in the bottom of the yogurt pots and thread the string through until the knot is inside the pot.
2 Put the breadcrumbs etc into the bowl.
3 Gently melt the lard in the saucepan and then pour it on to the ingredients in the bowl. An adult should pour hot fat.

4 Stir the mixture thoroughly until everything is well coated with fat and then spoon it into the prepared yogurt pots. Press the mixture down quite firmly.
5 Wait until the cakes have set before taking them into the garden to hang up for the birds.

A snowman

Collect together:

- 3 sheets of black paper: one 10cm by 10cm, one 5cm by 10cm, one 2cm by 10cm
- a toilet roll tube
- cotton wool
- glue and a glue brush
- a tiny piece of red paper
- a small straight twig about 15cm long
- scissors

To make your snowman

1 Cut two small holes on opposite sides of the tube, about 3cm from one end. Then push the twig through the holes, so that it sticks out equally on each side. This will form the snowman's arms.
2 Using the glue and the cotton wool, cover the tube with 'snow'.
3 Take the 5cm by 10cm piece of black paper and cut out six tiny circles. Stick these into position using two for eyes, one for a nose and three as buttons.
4 Cut out a small mouth from the red paper and stick it on to the Snowman.
5 Now to make his hat. Take the 10cm by 10cm piece of black paper, cut out a circle, slightly larger than the top of the Snowman's body, and stick this on top of the Snowman. Make a tube shape with the 2cm by 10cm piece of black paper and stick this on top of the black paper circle.

A cracker of home-made bath salts

Collect together:

- a toilet roll tube
- a small piece of cling film
- a piece of pretty wrapping paper, 21cm by 30cm
- Sellotape
- 2 rubber bands
- a teaspoon
- baking-soda
- washing-soda
- an egg cup
- a beaker
- a shallow bowl

To make your bath salts

1 Dissolve a small level teaspoon of baking-soda in the beaker with an egg-cupful of warm (not hot) water.
2 When the baking-soda has dissolved, add four teaspoons of powdered washing-soda and dissolve this in the mixture.
3 Pour the mixture into the shallow bowl and set it in a warm place until the water has evaporated and the salt crystals have formed.

To make the cracker

1 Take the small handful of bath salts and wrap them in the cling film. Put the wrapped bath salts inside the toilet roll tube.
2 Wrap the pretty paper round the tube, making sure that an equal amount of paper overlaps each end of the tube. Then sellotape the paper into position.
3 Tie up both ends of the cracker with a rubber band. The cracker can be decorated with a small picture cut out from an old Christmas card and stuck on to the tube. Alternatively, a simple bow of ribbon could be tied on.

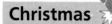

A snow storm

Collect together:

- 1 empty screw-top jar with lid
- 2 tablespoons of waterproof filler
- plastic cake decorations, such as a robin or Father Christmas
- a tube of silver glitter

To make your snowstorm

1 Mix up the filler and put it in the bottom of the jar. Wipe away any filler that clings to the side of the jar, or the snow storm will be hidden.
2 While the filler is still wet, put the Christmas decoration in position and allow the filler to dry completely.
3 Fill the jar with cold water and a generous sprinkle of silver glitter. The glitter will form the snow. Screw the lid back on to the jar.
4 Shake well and put up your umbrella!

An angel

Collect together:

- 1 toilet roll tube
- tinfoil approx 18cm by 18cm
- glue and a glue brush
- 1 paper doily, either white or silver
- a piece of white paper approx 6cm by 6cm
- scissors
- a felt-tip pen
- Sellotape

To make your angel

1 Wrap the tinfoil tightly round the tube and sellotape it into position. Tuck the loose ends of the tinfoil into the top and bottom of the tube.
2 Glue the doily into position behind the tube. If you find that the doily is too big then cut it in half.

3 Cut out a circle from the white paper. Draw a pretty face on the circle with the felt tip pen.
4 Glue the face on to the toilet roll.
5 You could hang a group of these angels together in a corner of the room to make a very attractive Christmas mobile.

A stained-glass window Christmas card

Collect together:

- a sheet of stiff coloured card, 20cm by 15cm
- a sheet of thin white paper, 20cm by 15cm
- felt-tip pens
- glue and a glue brush
- scissors
- a small piece of cotton wool
- a little cooking oil
- a piece of ribbon, 15cm long
- Sellotape

To make the card

1 Draw an arched window shape on the front of the sheet of card and cut it out with the scissors.
2 Using the cut out window as a template, draw the window on to the thin white paper.
3 Create a Christmas design inside the window on the paper. Carefully colour the picture with the felt-tip pens.
4 Cut the coloured window out, but be sure to leave a small border all the way round the outside.
5 Rub a little cooking oil all over the reverse of the drawing with the cotton wool.
6 Stick the coloured window into position behind the cut out card.
7 When the glue has dried, write a Christmas message on the back of the card. Sellotape a loop of ribbon to the top of the card and pop it into a large envelope. The recipient can hang the card in a window where the daylight will shine through the picture.

Valentine's Day

Fruit painting

Liquidise either tinned or fresh fruit, e.g. strawberries, blackcurrants and peaches. Put the different purees into separate bowls.

Give each child a large white plate, a small teaspoon and a cocktail or ice-lolly stick. Ask the children to create pictures with the fruit puree by dribbling different coloured puree on to the plate and swirling the colours together with the cocktail stick. As it's Valentine's Day, large hearts and flowers might be appropriate.

The finished pictures look good enough to eat – and of course they can be, with a blob of ice-cream on top.

My favourite things

Raindrops on roses and *whiskers on kittens* were two of the favourite things mentioned in a well-known song.

Ask your child to create a list of his or her very own favourite things. You might be surprised by some of the items included on the list. When the list is completed it could be turned into a poem.

And remember, it's not only your child's paintings which can be displayed, creative writing should be attractively 'shown off' as well.

Design some family stamps

If your child is delivering her Valentine cards by hand she could personalise the envelopes with family stamps.

It isn't only the royal family who can be immortalised on a stamp. Your child can have great fun designing and cutting out stamps which contain the portraits of members of her own family, including the family dog.

Large squared graph paper is very useful as it

is already marked out but failing this, stamp sized squares can be drawn directly on to paper.

This activity might serve as a general introduction to the use of stamps which later might lead on to an interest in stamp collecting.

Perhaps they could even write to the "Stamp Bug Club" which provides all sorts of stamp collecting information.

Stamp Bug Club
Freepost
PO BOX 109
Baker St
High Wycombe
Buckinghamshire
HP11 2TD

The take-a-letter game

Here is a game most suitable for a Valentine party.

Print some lower-case letters on individual pieces of card. On a separate sheet of paper make a list of the letters you have used and beside each one write a Valentine instruction or question, e.g.

a. Kiss the person on your left
b. Sing a well known love song
c. Name five famous couples, e.g. Victoria and Albert

Place the cards letter side up at one end of the room and stand with the children and the list of instructions on the opposite side of the room.

Using the minute hand on your watch give each child a set time in which to fetch one letter at a time and carry out the instructions. When his time is up he keeps the letters he has collected and the next player takes a turn.

The winner is the one with the most letters.

Who are you going to marry?

Give each person playing this game a long strip of paper and a pencil. Ask everyone to fold the paper into four equal sections by folding the paper in half and then in half again.

Without looking at each other's work, ask everyone to draw a head on the first section of the paper. The heads can be ugly, funny, happy or sad. Make sure that the neck protrudes slightly into the next section.

When everyone has finished the head they fold the paper over so that the head can't be seen but the neck is just visible. You then exchange papers with each other and draw a body in the next section of the paper. After folding and exchanging papers again, the legs and feet are drawn and finally in the last section you write down the name of a famous or well-known person. The papers are exchanged for the last time and unwrapped.

Your child now has the picture and name of the person she is going to marry!

Dream cups

Collect together:

- a plastic egg box
- cooking chocolate
- cake crumbs
- natural orange juice
- raisins
- a banana
- a bowl
- 2 teaspoons
- a knife
- a double boiler or small saucepan

To make the dream cups

1 Melt the chocolate in the double boiler or saucepan.
2 Use the teaspoon to coat the inside cups of the plastic egg box with the melted chocolate. You may have to do this several times in order to build up a satisfactory depth of chocolate.
3 While the chocolate cups are cooling, mix together the cake crumbs and raisins with sufficient orange juice to make a moist mixture.

4 When the chocolate has hardened, peel off the platic egg box and fill each cup with the cake crumb mixture.
5 Peel and slice the banana. Put a slice of banana on top of each chocolate cup.

Bread flowers for a Valentine posy

Ask your child to wash her hands.

Now take a small piece from a slice of white bread and ask her to mould and knead it with her fingers until the bread becomes smooth, pliable and rather like Plasticine or 'dough.

Take a small piece of the bread dough (about the size of a pea) and squash this between two fingers. This will make a petal shape.

Several petals can be made to form a flower shape by gently licking the base of each one and carefully pressing the petals together.

Leave the flowers to dry out and harden for a few hours and then paint them with nail varnish.

A pressed-flower posy

There are two ways of pressing and preserving flowers.

a. Line a dish with blotting paper. Place a layer of silver sand in the dish. Arrange the flowers on the sand and then cover them with a second layer of sand. Leave the dish in a warm airing cupboard for a month.

b. Place the flowers between layers of kitchen towel roll or newspaper. Put some heavy weights on top and leave them for several weeks.

Collect together:

- a selection of pressed flowers
- a small paper doily
- a sheet of coloured card 20cm by 20cm
- a small length of pretty ribbon
- a pair of compasses with a pencil
- scissors
- glue and a glue brush

To make the posy

1 Using the compasses, draw a circle on the card exactly the same size as the doily. Cut out the circle of card.
2 Glue the doily on to the card circle.
3 Make a small loop with the ribbon and glue this on to the back of the circle of card, making sure that the loop stands above the edge of the circle.
4 Arrange the flowers in the centre of the doily and then very carefully glue them into position.

If the posy is being given as a Valentine present, a suitable message could be written on the back of the card.

Love heart earrings

Cut two heart shapes from thick white card and help your child to decorate both sides of the hearts with glitter, sequins, tiny beads, enamel paint or felt-tip pen.

Using scissors, make a small hole near the top of each heart and loop a small length of string through the holes. The loop needs to be large enough to fit comfortably over the top of your child's ear.

Pink dream mousse

Collect together:

- 2 raspberry jellies
- 300ml (half a pint) of boiling water
- 250g marshmallows
- 2 x 400g cans of evaporated milk. Keep in the refrigerator before use
- 280ml (half a pint) of whipped cream
- kitchen scissors
- a whisk, either hand or electric
- 2 mixing bowls
- a pretty serving bowl
- a wooden spoon

To make the mousse

1 Dissolve the jellies in the boiling water. Leave the liquid in the mixing bowl to cool (but not so long that it sets).
2 Cut 8 of the marshmallows in half and snip the rest into little pieces.
3 Whisk the evaporated milk until it is thick. Add the cool jelly, the whipped cream and the pieces of marshmallow. Pour the mixture into the serving bowl and place it in the refrigerator until it is set.
4 Before serving, decorate the mousse with the remaining halved marshmallows.

A Valentine card

Collect together:

- a sheet of coloured card, 40cm by 20cm
- a small paper doily
- a piece of shiny red paper 9cm by 9cm
- silver glitter
- a felt-tip pen
- scissors
- glue and a glue brush

To make the card

1 Fold the card in half so that the front measures 20cm by 20cm. Write a Valentine message inside.
2 Glue the doily on to the front of the card. Put small drops of glue into the holes around the outside edge of the doily and then sprinkle these with the silver glitter. Shake off any excess glitter.
3 Cut out a heart shape from the shiny red paper and glue this on to the centre of the doily.

Make-up sessions and dressing up

On this one special day of the year why not open the wardrobe doors and allow the children to try on your clothes and shoes. You could stipulate that everything has to be returned neatly afterwards. Put out some of your old make-up and perhaps an inexpensive bottle of perfume and provide lots of cotton wool and make-up removing cream.

A bracelet

Suggest that your child paints some macaroni with enamel paints or coloured nail varnish. When the pasta has dried it can be threaded on to elasticated thread to form a bracelet.

Chocolate fruit

Collect together:

- a selection of fruit, such as an apple, a pear and a banana
- a knife
- cocktail sticks
- 1 bar of cooking chocolate
- a double boiler or a small saucepan
- sugar strands or similar tiny sweets
- a plate
- a saucer
- a wire cooling rack

To make the chocolate fruit

1 Cut the washed fruit into chunks and spear each piece with a cocktail stick.
2 Put the tiny sweets on the saucer.
3 Melt the chocolate in the double boiler or saucepan and bring it to the table. Obviously very young children shouldn't handle hot pans. Hold the saucepan steady, dip each piece of fruit into the chocolate and then sprinkle them with the tiny sweets.
4 Place the fruit on a wire rack to set.

A flower salad

Collect together:

- a small lettuce
- spring onions
- 2 tomatoes
- 3 new carrots
- 6 radishes
- ice cubes
- French salad dressing
- a vegetable parer
- a small sharp knife
- a large bowl full of iced water
- 2 spoons
- a pretty bowl for serving the salad
- a plate

To make the flower salad

1 Remove the outer leaves from the lettuce. Separate the remaining leaves and wash them if they seem dirty. Leave the leaves on one side.
2 Trim and wash the spring onions.

3 Wash the tomatoes and cut them into quarters. Place them on the plate in the refrigerator.
4 Using the vegetable parer, thinly pare the carrots. Place the thin strips of carrot in the iced water and add more ice cubes. After a little while, the carrot will start to curl up.
5 Trim the radishes and with a sharp knife make three cuts trom the tip to the stalk end. Do not cut all the way through the radish but stop just before you reach the bottom. Place the radishes in the iced water and they will open out to look remarkably like flowers.
6 When all the vegetables are ready put the lettuce, tomatoes and spring onions into the pretty bowl. Toss them with the salad dressing. Drain the carrot curls and radish roses and use these to decorate the salad.

An orange peel necklace

Help your child to peel some oranges by first cutting the skin into quarters. Take a sharp knife and cut some interesting shapes out of the peel, e.g. diamonds, triangles, squares.

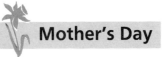

Using a knife or a knitting needle, make a hole in a corner of each shape. (The shapes need to be fairly big to make this possible.)

Place the shapes in the airing cupboard to dry out and harden. This will take a couple of weeks. When they are ready your child can make a necklace by threading the shapes on to thin ribbon or elasticated thread.

Perfumed pictures

Ask your child to draw a simple picture on a sheet of paper, e.g. a vase of flowers or a simple landscape. Collect together some ingredients which have a pleasant smell. These could include talcum powder, ground cinnamon, ground cloves, dried thyme, dried rosemary, etc.

Cover one section of the picture at a time with a thin layer of glue and then sprinkle the glue with one of the smells. Shake off any excess powder and start gluing the next section.

A sweet smeller

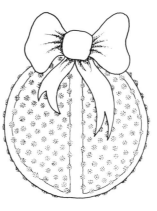

Collect together:

- an orange or lemon
- a length of ribbon
- pins
- cloves
- tissue paper
- a knitting needle
- orris root powder

To make a sweet smeller

1 Wrap the ribbon round the fruit so that it is divided into quarters. Pin the ribbon into position.
2 Using the knitting needle, make small holes in the exposed skin of the fruit and then press a whole clove into each hole.
3 Remove the ribbon. Roll the fruit in a few spoons of the orris root powder. (This helps to preserve the smell but it could be omitted.) Then wrap the fruit in some tissue paper and place the sweet smeller in a warm place, such as an airing cupboard, for three weeks.
4 After three weeks, unwrap the sweet smeller, replace the ribbon and tie a bow on the top.

A daffodil Mother's Day card

Collect together:

- an empty egg box
- scissors
- yellow paint
- green paint
- 2 paint brushes
- glue and a glue brush
- a sheet of card 40cm by 24cm
- a felt-tip pen

To make the card

1 Fold the sheet of card in half so that the front of the card measures 20cm by 24cm. Write a Mother's Day message inside the card.
2 On the front of the card paint some green leaves and yellow petals. As the 'trumpet' part of the daffodil will be created from the eggbox it is only necessary to paint the outside petals of each daffodil. You should aim to make each flower approx 6cm wide.

3 Cut out the cups from the eggbox (you will need as many as you have flowers on the card) and paint them yellow.
4 When the eggbox cups have dried, stick them hollow side up, in the centre of each petal shape.

A little ballerina

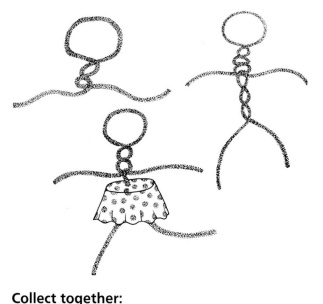

Collect together:

- 2 pipe cleaners
- a paper cake case

To make the ballerina

1 Use the illustration as a guide. Twist the first pipe cleaner to form a head and two arms.
2 Thread the second pipe cleaner through the bottom loop in the first pipe cleaner and then twist it to form the body and legs.
3 Push the paper cake case on to the pipe cleaners in order to form the ballerina's skirt.

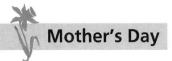

A Mother's Day picture poem

Here is your child's chance to be perfectly honest about all of mum's attributes, good and bad!

Suggest that your child draws mum's face on a piece of paper. The face shouldn't have any hair drawn around it. The hair itself should be formed by writing out a list of words which the child associates with mum. As you can see from the illustration, if mum's hair is curly the writing can be drawn in curved lines.

Washing the car

Provide the children with large buckets of soapy water, lots of sponges, a hose pipe connected to the cold water tap, and the car. Make sure that all the car windows are tightly closed and leave them to it.

Now dash into the house and read the Sunday newspapers with a cup of coffee. How long dare you leave it before you go outside to check how things are going?

Easter

Decorating eggs

Hard boil or blow lots of eggs and let your child's artistic skills flourish by providing the following:

- paints
- very fine paint brushes
- felt-tip pens
- glue and a glue brush
- sequins
- thin ribbon and wool
- very thin cardboard

As you can see from the illustration, all sorts of exciting faces and patterns can be produced. Blown eggs are, however, rather fragile so with younger children it is probably better to provide hard-boiled eggs.

An Easter egg treasure hunt

Make finding the Easter egg part of the fun by laying a trail of written clues around the home and garden. On pieces of paper write out some instructions such as,

"Look in the coldest part of the house". (The fridge)

On looking in the fridge the child would find the next clue which could say,

"Look under the – – d". (Bed)

Finally the last clue should indicate where the Easter egg can be found.

An Easter mobile

Help your child to make a simple coat hanger mobile by cutting out some Easter shapes from card, for example, a rabbit, a lamb, a chick, a spring flower, and an egg.

The shapes can be decorated either with felt-tip pens and paints or with crushed tissue paper and other collage materials.

Make a hole in the top of each shape with a pair of scissors and attach them to the coat hanger with varying lengths of strong cotton thread.

A decorated Easter cake

Ask your child to collect some tiny springtime flowers, e.g. primroses or violets, and paint them with egg white. Sprinkle the flowers with caster sugar. Gently shake off any excess sugar and leave the flowers to dry out on greaseproof paper.

The flowers can be used by the child to decorate the top of an iced sponge cake and for a special finish, you could also tie a bow of yellow ribbon around the outside of the cake.

A patch of garden

Easter is traditionally the time when people start to think about the garden and children benefit enormously from having a small patch of garden of their own. The vegetables they grow can be eaten by the whole family and any flowers they produce can not only decorate the house but be given away as presents.

At this time of year the garden should be prepared for planting. Give each child a carrier bag and set a little competition to see who can remove the most stones and weeds. After digging over the garden, a trip to the local garden centre to select seeds and seedlings is always exciting.

On returning home, follow the instructions on the back of the seed packets and help your child by reminding him to regularly water and weed his plot of garden.

The following list of recommended plants is quite long but it is probably better for your child to grow only one or two vegetables, and two different types of flowers at any one time. Any more than this and the exercise can become rather complicated.

The list suggests some of the most suitable plants for children to grow. These plants thrive with comparatively little effort and annuals (plants which flower the same year they are planted) are best for children, as the child doesn't have to wait two years for results.

Vegetables: potatoes, carrots, lettuce, peas, runner-beans, radish, marrow.
Flowers: aster, pansy, antirrhinum, nasturtium, marigold, sunflower, sweet-pea, petunia, lobelia.

You may also like to visit a garden which is open to the public. They are often breathtakingly beautiful when the early spring flowers are blooming. For details of over 1,500 gardens which are open to the public write to,

The National Gardens Scheme
57 Lower Belgrave St
London
SW1 0LR

Growing seeds, pips and stones

Children don't necessarily need a garden in order to grow plants. Almost any seed, pip or fruit stone can be successfully germinated within the home.

Mustard and cress seed

Germinate on damp cotton wool and water as necessary.

Dried peas or broad beans

Line a jam jar with damp blotting paper. Soak peas and beans overnight before placing them in between the blotting paper and the jar. Water as necessary to keep the blotting paper damp.

Bean-sprouts, either mung or aduki beans

Place a couple of spoonfuls of the beans in a large, empty glass coffee jar. Cover the top of the jar with a clean handkerchief and hold this in position with an elastic band.

Pour enough water through the handkerchief to cover the beans. Leave the beans to soak for twelve hours. Empty the water out of the jar without removing the handkerchief and place the jar in a dark place.

Each day water the beans and then immediately drain off the water through the handkerchief.

The beans take about a week to grow and can then be used in salads and stir-fry dishes.

Peach and plum stones

Gently crack these slightly with a nutcracker and then plant them in a pot of damp compost. Cover the pot with a plastic bag and then place in a warm, dark place. Water as necessary and expect to see some shoots in about two to three weeks.

The top slice from a fresh pineapple

A pineapple top, with as much of the flesh removed as possible, should be left to lie on its side to dry out for a few days before being planted in damp sand.

Date stones

These can be planted straight into a pot of moist compost.

Orange and lemon pips

Can be planted into pots of damp compost. Water well and leave the pots in a dark, warm place. The pips will take several weeks to germinate, so do remember to keep adding water.

An onion bottle

Many children have grown carrot tops in a saucer of water, but you don't have to restrict this activity to the humble carrot. The top from any root vegetable, if placed in water, will put out shoots within a few days. So why not grow a swede, parsnip, beetroot or turnip top?

Avocado stones (soaked in water for two days first) or an onion, if placed with their rounded end in the top of a bottle of water, will also eventually produce roots and leaves.

Do make sure that your child checks the bottle regularly to ensure that the root end is always covered in water.

When there are plenty of roots the avocado or onion could be transferred to a flower pot full of damp potting compost. The compost should come about half way up the stone or onion and eventually the plant may also need a thin cane to support it as it grows.

Grow a picture

Place a large sheet of blotting paper on to a tray or baking sheet. Using a black crayon, ask your child to draw an animal on to the paper. A hedgehog is rather a good subject for the picture.

Make the blotting paper damp with water and then sprinkle mustard and cress seeds on to the appropriate parts of the animals body. For example, the hedgehog's face and paws can be left empty and the seeds sprinkled on his body.

Keep the paper damp and after a few days the seeds will sprout and look remarkably like the hedgehog's spines.

Easter bonnets

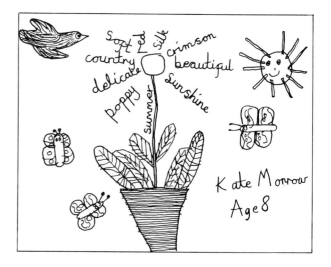

Collect together:

- plain digestive biscuits
- icing sugar
- different food colourings
- a jug of hot water
- a bowl for mixing
- a dessertspoon
- a teaspoon
- a quantity of sugar flower sweets, small sweets, glace cherries etc.
- a packet of marshmallows
- a wire cooling rack
- a knife

To make the bonnets

1 Put a heaped dessertspoon of icing sugar in a bowl and add the hot water, a little at a time, until the mixture is smooth but not too runny. Add a little food colouring.
2 Using a teaspoon, spread a little of the icing sugar mixture over the top of a digestive biscuit. The icing needs to be quite thickly spread or the decorations will drop off.
3 In the middle of the iced biscuit place a marshmallow. This will form the crown of the bonnet. Around the crown arrange the sugar flowers or sweets.

4 Make several of the bonnets using different coloured icing and sweets and then leave them to set hard on the wire cooling rack.

A flower petal poem

Give your child a flower to look at, touch and smell. Ask her to think of and make a list of words which describe her feelings as she discovers the flower. Younger children will need a little help in formulating their list. You can help them to describe their feelings by asking questions such as, "What does the smell remind you of?" When the child has made a list of about ten words she can create her flower petal poem.

To do this she will need a sheet of paper 20cm by 20cm and a felt-tip pen or pencil. At the bottom of the paper, draw a simple flower pot with a stalk and leaves growing from the pot. The flower itself is created by drawing a circle and surrounding the circle with the collection of words, the words forming the petals of the flower.

An Easter rabbit card

Collect together:

- a sheet of card 40 cm by 24cm
- a felt tip pen
- crayons
- scissors
- an egg box
- glue and a glue brush
- a few small sugar or chocolate eggs

To make the card

1 Fold the card in half so that the front of the card measures 20cm by 24cm. Write an Easter message inside the card.
2 On the front of the card draw the outline shape of a large rabbit. Colour the rabbit in with the crayons.
3 Take the scissors and carefully cut out one of the cups from the egg box.
4 Glue the cup on to the front of the card so that it looks rather like the bottom half of a shopping basket. It obviously needs to be positioned near to the rabbits paws.
5 To make the shopping bag look more realistic, use the felt tip pen to draw a handle above the egg cup.
6 When the egg cup has dried, put a few small eggs inside it.

Egg shell heads

Collect together:

- empty egg shells
- felt tip pens
- soil
- mustard and cress seed
- 1 teaspoon
- 1 empty egg box
- scissors

To make the egg heads

1 Cut out the cups from the empty egg box.
2 Stand an empty egg shell in each cup, open side upwards, and draw a face on each shell with the felt tip pens. You could also draw buttons and pockets on the cups to represent the body.
3 Gently spoon a little soil into each shell and sprinkle it with seed. Make sure the soil doesn't dry out and soon the egg shell men will grow hair.

A spring flower posy

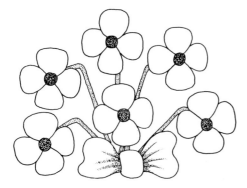

Collect together:

- a small ball of Plasticine
- 6 pipe cleaners (green ones would be nice)
- felt-tip pens or crayons
- a piece of card, 20cm by 20cm
- scissors

To make the posy

1 Draw six flower shapes on the piece of card. Cut the shapes out and colour them on both sides.
2 Make a small hole with the pointed end of the pair of scissors in the centre of each card flower.

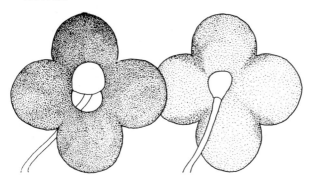

3 Push the pipe cleaners through the holes in the flowers, leaving about 1cm of pipe cleaner showing on top of each flower.
4 Take the Plasticine and make 12 tiny balls, two for each flower. One ball goes on top of the flower, pressed on to the pipe cleaner. The second one should be pressed around the pipe cleaner just underneath the flower. Bend the pipe cleaners slightly for a more natural effect.

Marzipan animals

Collect together:

- 50g hard margarine
- 50g caster sugar
- 250g Madeira cake crumbs
- 2 teaspoons almond essence
- currants
- almonds
- edible silver balls
- food colour
- fine paint brushes
- a small amount of flour

To make mock marzipan

Cream together the margarine and sugar. Add the cake crumbs and the almond essence and work the mixture with your fingers until it forms a marzipan-like ball. Alternatively you can buy ready made marzipan.

To create animals

Take small lumps of the marzipan and on a lightly floured surface mould the marzipan to create Easter chicks, rabbits and lambs. Eyes can be made from the currants or silver balls, ears from the almonds and, for a really special finish, the animals could be painted with food colouring.

Father's Day

Father's whiskers picture poem

Ask your child to make a list of words which he associates with dad, e.g. happy, funny, bad-tempered, newspaper, jogging, Mars bars.

Having drawn dad's face on a sheet of paper, the child could go on to use the words in place of the whiskers on dad's chin. The words need to be printed as small as possible in order to get a whiskery effect.

Of course if dad just happens to have a beard or a moustache, lots of words will be needed!

Soap carving

Dad might have to help at times with this activity which is only really suitable for older children.

Using a felt-tip pen, ask your child to draw the outline shape of an animal or object on to the back and front of a large tablet of soap. (A paper template helps tremendously when doing this.)

Now with a knife or a potato peeler cut away at the soap until the outline shape emerges. Fine details can now be carved into the object using a smaller knife.

The carving is smoothed by gently rubbing it in a bowl of warm water. Finally take it out of the water and let the soap dry. Add further fine details by scratching the surface of the soap with a cocktail stick. The carving can be polished by rubbing it with a little cooking oil.

A piggy bank

Help your child to take an empty washing-up liquid bottle and cut off the top. You should be left with a cylindrical box. Cut a small hole for the money to go through, in the side of the cylinder.

Take a circle of paper and an elastic band. Press the paper over the open end of the cylinder and hold it in position with the elastic band.

Turn the cylinder on its side with the money slit at the top and glue the final details into position.

Four corks for legs, a cork for a nose, a curly pipe-cleaner tail, and ears made from stiff paper or card. The eyes can be drawn on to the pig with a felt-tip pen.

An express train tea

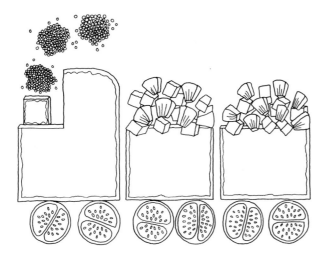

placing the slices of tomato underneath the bread. The smoke coming from the chimney can be produced with a few spoons of cottage cheese and the ham and pineapple looks very tempting when placed in the trucks.

Cheese rockets

Collect together:

- 2 slices of bread and butter
- cottage cheese
- cubes of ham
- a few pineapple chunks (well drained)
- 6 thin slices of tomato
- a large plate
- a knife
- a teaspoon

Collect together:

- a knife
- a chopping board
- 10 long wooden kebab sticks
- pineapple chunks (well drained)
- 5 small tomatoes, cut in half
- 125g button mushrooms
- 10 rashers of streaky bacon with rind removed
- 250g cheddar cheese

To make the train

1 Cut the crusts from the bread. Cut one slice in half and cut away a quarter of the second slice. Cut out a small rectangle from the quarter slice. This will be used as the chimney of the engine.
2 Place the bread and butter on the plate. Create your express train by using the three quarter slices as the engine (don't forget the chimney) and the two half slices as the trucks.
3 The wheels on the train can be created by

To make the rockets

1 Cut 75g of cheese into 10 cubes. Cut the rest of the cheese into 10 triangles.
2 Cut the rashers of bacon in half. Wrap each rasher of bacon round a chunk of pineapple.
3 Push a bacon roll on to each kebab stick. Then add one tomato half and a button mushroom. Finally top each stick with a second bacon roll. Grill the kebabs until cooked.
4 Place a cube of cheese followed by a triangle of cheese on the top of every kebab.

A Father's Day card

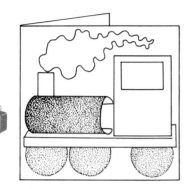

Collect together:

- a sheet of card 44cm by 15cm
- a toilet roll tube
- a piece of sticky backed coloured paper 11cm by 11cm. If you can't obtain sticky backed paper, plain coloured paper would do.
- felt-tip pens or crayons
- glue and a glue brush
- scissors
- cotton wool

To make the card

1 Fold the sheet of card in half so that the front of the card measures 22cm by 15cm. Write a Father's day message inside.
2 Cut the toilet roll tube in half along its length. Using the sticky backed paper cover the outside of the half tube. If you are using ordinary paper, cover the half tube with glue and stick the paper into position.
3 Glue the covered tube on to the front of the card. This will form the boiler of a train engine.
4 Using the felt-tip pens draw and colour in the chimney above the boiler, the wheels, and the engine driver's cab.

5 Dab a little glue above the chimney and add some cotton wool smoke.

A pen tidy for dad's desk

Collect together:

- a toilet roll tube
- a sheet of pretty paper, 17cm by 24cm
- a piece of card, 10cm by 10cm
- glue and a glue brush
- a new pen or pencil
- Sellotape

To make the tidy

1 Wrap the pretty paper round the tube and sellotape it into position. Tuck the loose ends of the paper into the top and bottom of the tube.
2 Glue one end of the tube and press it on to the piece of card. When the tube has dried in this position, pop the new pen into its new holder.

If you are feeling really ambitious, several tubes could be stuck together on a larger piece of card so that dad can keep rulers, pencils and all sorts of things tidy.

Tail on the cat

Instead of a donkey draw a black cat (minus tail) on a large sheet of paper. Make a mark where the tail should be found.

Give each player a length of black wool attached to a small piece of Blu-Tack and, with eyes blindfolded, ask the children to place the cat's tail in the correct position. The winner is the one to place the wool nearest to the mark.

Shadow puppets

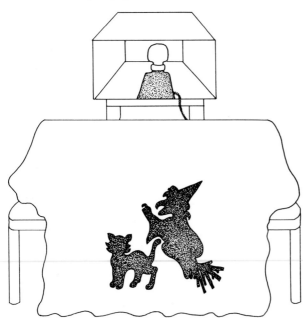

To make the theatre your child will need:

- a large white sheet
- three kitchen chairs
- adhesive tape
- a large cardboard box lined with tin foil
- a small table lamp with the shade removed

To make the puppets your child will need:

- some thick cardboard (you could use empty grocery boxes)
- a felt-tip pen
- Sellotape
- scissors
- a few thin garden canes

To create the theatre:

Stand two of the kitchen chairs next to each other with a gap of about 130cm between them. Spread the sheet between the chairs and tape it into position. Place the third chair directly behind the sheet, approximately 75cm away.

Put the lamp into the cardboard box. (The box needs to be large enough for there to be a safe distance between the bulb and the cardboard.) Stand the box and lamp on the third chair so that the open side of the box and the lamp are facing the sheet.

To create the puppets:

Draw some silhouette figures for the play on the thick cardboard. The figures need to be at least 30cm high. Cut the figures out and attach the canes to the back of each silhouette with some Sellotape.

To stage the play

Switch out the main lights or draw the curtains. Switch on the table lamp in the box and hold the puppets very close to the sheet. Because the light is behind the puppets, the audience will be able to see the puppet shadows through the sheet.

The mystery of the darkness and these shadow puppets really catches the atmosphere of Halloween.

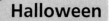
Abracadabra

Creating magic words, invocations and spells can be a great source of fun and amusement for your child.

Here are a few "spells" and "witch poems" to read to your child before she creates her own.

Hinx, minx
The old witch winks,
The fat begins to fry.
There's nobody home
But jumping Joan,
Father, mother and I.

(Traditional)

Double, double toil and trouble
Fire burn and cauldron bubble.
Fillet of a fenny snake,
In the cauldron boil and bake;
Eye of newt and toe of frog,
Wool of bat and tongue of dog,
Adder's fork and blind worms sting.
For a charm of powerful trouble
Like a hell-broth boil and bubble.

(Shakespeare)

See a slit eyed witch
With a pointed nose.
Two pointed ears
and claws for her toes.

She sits on her broom
And looks at you,
And flaps her cloak
And cries WHOO-HOO!

(Traditional)

A witch's hat

Give the children a sheet of black paper, Sellotape and scissors.

Ask them to make a witch's hat. They can best do this by drawing an arc across the paper, then cutting the paper and curling it into a conical shape before sellotaping it into position.

The hat could be decorated with silver tinfoil stars and crescent moons and the children could stick black or green wool hair on the inside brim.

Hunting the ghost

This game is played in the dark.

Taking turns, one of the players dresses as the ghost by placing an old sheet over his head. (Cut out holes in the sheet for eyes.) The ghost then goes into another room to hide.

The remaining players then search the house for the ghost. The ghost can help a little by making spooky noises. The searchers take a torch with them but they are only allowed to quickly flash the torch ten times. If they are able to "catch" the ghost directly in the beam of the torch another player takes a turn at being the ghost. If after ten flashes the ghost hasn't been caught, he wins a small prize and the game continues with another player as ghost.

The cauldron game

This memory game is very suitable for a party.

To make the cauldron, cover a round washing basket with black paper or, alternatively, use a cardboard grocery box.

Make a collection of lots of objects, e.g. a toy spider, a carrot, a candle, a sugar mouse etc. (Make sure that the children don't see the objects.)

Give each child a pencil and paper and ask them to watch while you drop one item at a time into the cauldron. The number of items used rather depends on the age of the children involved. As you drop the objects into the basket you could make the spell complete by saying some magic words.

When you have finished making the spell, ask the children to remember and to write down the ingredients. The winner is the first one to write down a complete list.

Black spells

This game (for older children) should be played in complete darkness and needs to be prepared secretly before the party starts.

An adult should make a collection of objects which "feel" like the possible ingredients for a spell, e.g.

- a spider (four pipe-cleaners twisted together)
- a dead frog's leg (a finger cut from an old rubber-glove)
- a dead man's finger (a carrot)
- an eye (a peeled boiled egg)
- a mouse (a cotton wool ball)

Ask the party guests to sit in a circle and turn out the lights. Carefully explain what each item is before passing it round the circle. Make the explanations as blood-curdling as you like, and be prepared for lots of screams!

Ice-cream witches

a comfit for her nose and a jelly bean for her mouth. Sprinkle hundreds and thousands over the top and sides of the ball to form the witch's hair.

3 Pop an ice-cream cone hat on top of each witches head and serve immediately.

The witch's nose

Collect together:

- chocolate biscuits
- a tub of easy scoop ice-cream
- ice-cream cones
- Smarties
- jelly beans
- liquorice comfits
- hundreds and thousands
- an ice-cream scoop
- a saucer for each witch you are going to make

To make a witch

You will have to work quickly, so have all your ingredients ready before you start.

1 Place a chocolate biscuit in the middle of a saucer. Put a round scoop of ice-cream on the biscuit.
2 Using the sweets, create a witch's face on the ice-cream ball. Place two Smarties for her eyes,

Help your child to draw a witch's profile, minus nose, on a sheet of card.

Make two small holes in the profile, one on each side of the gap where the nose should be. Take an unwanted chain from a necklace and push each end of the chain through the holes in the card. The length of the chain hanging down should be about double the width of the space for the nose.

Sellotape the chain into position on the underside of the card. The card can now be tilted and shaken to make the chain form many different witch noses.

A witch's brew

Collect together:

- 1 litre of ginger beer
- 250ml lemon squash
- 650ml soda water
- green food colouring
- slices of lemon
- a saucer of caster sugar
- a small bowl of whipped-up egg white
- a large jug
- drinking glasses
- bendy straws
- a wire cooling rack

To make the brew

1 Dip the rim of each glass first into the egg white and then into the caster sugar. Set the glasses on one side to dry and harden.
2 Dip the top half of each bendy straw into the egg white and then into the caster sugar. Put the straws on a wire cooling rack to set.

3 In the large jug, mix together the ginger beer, lemon squash and soda water. Add sufficient green food colouring to turn the drink into an evil looking concoction.
4 When serving, carefully pour the brew into a sugar frosted glass and add a slice of lemon and a sugar coated bendy straw.

Witch's fingers

Collect together:

- a pair of old green rubber gloves
- red nail varnish
- scissors
- glue and a glue brush
- thin card

To make the fingers

1 Cut off the fingers from the rubber gloves.
2 Cut out ten, long finger nail shapes from the card and paint each one with the red nail varnish.
3 When they are dry, glue the finger nails on to the rubber glove fingers.
4 When the glue has dried, slip the false fingers on to your fingers.

A paper witch

Collect together:

- a black paper semicircle, 20cm wide
- a circle of black paper, approx 9cm across
- a smaller circle of white paper about the size of a 5p coin
- felt-tip pens or crayons
- a few strands of green wool
- glue and a glue brush
- scissors

To make the witch

1 Take the black paper semicircle and glue it into a cone shape.
2 Cut a round hole in the middle of the black paper circle. The hole needs to be about 4cm wide.
3 Draw a nasty face on the small circle of white paper.
4 Gently push the point of the cone through the hole in the black paper circle. This will now look like a witch's pointed hat.

5 Glue the paper face underneath the hat.
6 Stick some green wool hair around the face and underneath the rim of the hat.

A spider

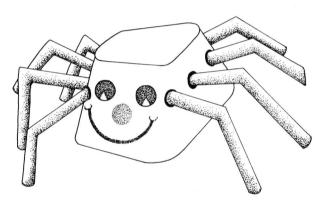

Collect together:

- an empty egg box
- 1 packet of pipe cleaners
- felt-tip pens
- scissors

To make the spider

1 Cut out one of the egg box cups.
2 Use the sharp point of the scissors to make eight tiny holes around the outside of the eggcup.
3 Use four pipe cleaners. Push each pipe cleaner through a hole on one side of the cup and out through a hole on the opposite side. Bend the pipe cleaners slightly to make them look more like spiders' legs.
4 Draw a spider's face on the front of the eggcup. Then, if you like, add a length of elasticated thread to the top of the cup so that the spider can bounce up and down.

Edible nasties

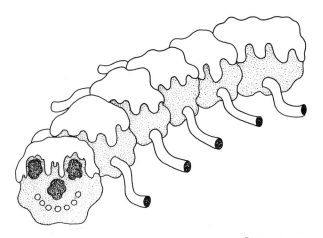

Collect together:

- 455g icing sugar
- 1 standard egg white
- lemon juice
- cornflour
- peppermint essence
- silver balls
- small pieces of clean string
- currants
- food colouring
- fine paint brushes
- a sieve
- a bowl
- a wooden spoon

To make the nasties

1 Sieve the icing sugar into the bowl. Add the egg white and mix together well with the wooden spoon.
2 With clean hands knead the mixture until it forms a ball. If it seems a little too dry and crumbly add a few drops of lemon juice. Add a few drops of peppermint essence.
3 On a surface sprinkled with corn flour, take small pieces of the mixture you have made and roll, squeeze, pinch and stretch it to create all sorts of nasties! These could be caterpillars, slugs, spiders, fingers, squashed flies and other such delightful inventions. To add to the fun, use the silver balls and currants for eyes, string for tails and the food colouring to paint such fine details as blood and slime.

A Halloween scratch picture

Using colourful wax crayons, ask your child if she would like to colour a sheet of paper with bands of colour.

When this has been completed, completely cover the coloured paper with black wax crayon.

The child then takes a cocktail stick or a sharp pencil and scratches a Halloween picture on to the paper. Where the black wax is scratched away the original colour will show through.

Be warned – this is a fairly messy activity.

Bonfire night

Make an un-guy

Many children are frightened by the sight of a guy being burnt on a bonfire, so why not encourage your child to make a guy for looking at or sitting on. The guy doesn't have to be male. A dress and tights can be stuffed with newspaper just as easily. Fasten the guy together with string and safety pins and make a head by drawing a face on a paper bag. Stuff the bag with newspapers and tie it to the top of the guy's body.

The guy race game

This is a game to play on your return indoors after the fireworks have finished.

At one end of the room put a pile of old clothes, some large paper bags (do remind young children never to use plastic bags for this game) and some felt-tip pens.

Divide the children into two teams and sit them as far away from the clothes as possible. At a given signal, one member from each team runs to the pile of clothes and puts something on, e.g. a pair of trousers or a dress. They then have to quickly draw a face on a paper bag, put the paper bag over their head and find their way back to their team. When they get back, the next team member runs to the clothes and so on.

The winning team is the first one with all its members dressed as guys.

A bonfire night safety poster

As adults we are aware of just how dangerous fireworks and bonfires can be if they are not treated with respect. To get this message across to your child in a fun way, why not suggest that he designs and paints a bonfire night safety poster.

Themes could include:

- never hold fireworks in your hand
- don't throw fireworks
- always keep a lid on the fireworks box
- don't carry fireworks in your pocket

The posters could be put up in your child's bedroom or you might find that your child's school would be more than happy to put a colourful poster on the school notice board.

A torn paper bonfire collage

Collect together:
- a sheet of black paper
- lots of brightly coloured paper (shiny paper is ideal)
- glue and a glue brush.

Ask your child to rip, not cut, the bright paper into flame shapes. Glue the shapes in overlapping layers on to the sheet of black paper.

A bonfire picture poem

To make this poem your child will need:

- a piece of black paper
- a pencil
- red, orange and yellow wax crayons
- glue and a glue brush
- variously coloured tubes of glitter

Help your child to think of a list of words which describe fireworks. Some of the words can be pure invention, e.g.

> sparkle, fizz, whizz, crackle, sprackle, whoosh.

On the bottom half of the black paper ask the child to use the wax crayons to draw some colourful flames curling and twisting into the night sky. In between the flames, and in the black sky above the flames, write out the firework words in pencil. The words need to have large letters but they don't need to be written in a straight line – some could be curved.

Carefully spread a little glue along the line of each letter and then sprinkle the letters with glitter. Shake off any excess glitter and your child should have a sparkling bonfire picture poem.

A rocket bottle

Help your child to find a large empty plastic bottle and a cork which will fit, not too tightly, into the top.

Stand the bottle on a tray or on the draining board in the kitchen. Put four dessert-spoonfuls of bicarbonate of soda into the bottle. Put ten dessert-spoonfuls of vinegar into a jug and then pour the vinegar on to the bicarbonate of soda. Quickly push the cork into the bottle and stand back!

Mixing bicarbonate with vinegar produces a gas (carbon-dioxide). The gas causes the mixture to foam and expand which pushes the cork out with quite a POP!

NB For obvious safety reasons, don't use a glass bottle, and don't use a cork which is too tight-fitting.

Bonfire masks

To make mask 1, collect together

- a large paper bag
- felt-tip pens, crayons or paints
- scissors

To make mask 2, collect together:

- a piece of card, 30cm by 21cm
- elasticated thread
- scissors
- Sellotape
- felt-tip pens
- glue and a glue brush
- milk bottle tops, wool, scraps of material

To make mask 1

Ask your child to draw or paint a face on the front of the paper bag and then to cut out two holes for eyes. Do remind younger children never to place plastic bags on their heads!

To make mask 2

Ask your child to cut out a simple mask shape, either full face or half face from the piece of card.

Cut out two eye holes and decorate the mask before attaching the elasticated thread. The decoration can include patterns drawn with the felt-tip pens or a collage effect can be produced by sticking on milk bottle tops and other objects.

Catherine wheels

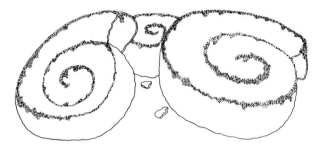

Collect together:

- 1 packet of frozen puff pastry (thawed)
- 1 jar of Marmite
- a blunt knife
- a small quantity of flour
- a rolling pin
- a flat baking tray
- a cooling rack

To make the catherine wheels

1 Roll out the pastry thinly on a floured surface.
2 With a knife, cut the pastry to make a rectangular shape, about 30cm by 20cm. Cut the rectangle into strips 4cm wide and then cut each strip in half.
3 Use the knife to spread the Marmite quite thinly over the top of each strip of pastry and then roll each strip up like a swiss roll.
4 Place the rolls of pastry on a baking tray and cook in the oven (gas mark 4, 180 C) for 20 minutes.

Potato bake

Collect together:

For each person
- 1 washed potato with its skin left on, sliced into three horizontal pieces
- 1 small onion peeled and sliced
- 1 carrot peeled and sliced
- a quarter pound hamburger
- salt
- 2 × 30cm squares of foil

To make the potato bake

1 In the centre of one of the layers of foil place the bottom slice of potato. On top of this place a slice of onion and two slices of carrot. Season them with a little salt. Place half the hamburger on top of the carrot and onion.
2 Continue with the next layer of potato, onion, carrot and hamburger, seasoning as each layer is added.

3 Finally place the last slice of potato on top.
4 Wrap the potato up tightly in the first layer of foil and then add a second layer of foil.
5 Put the potatoes in the very hot embers of the bonfire and bake them for one hour. Obviously an adult should be responsible for putting the potatoes into the embers and for removing them.

Chocolate leaves

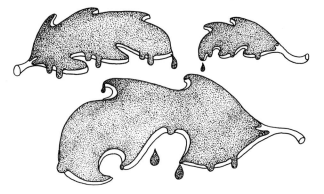

Collect together:

- cooking chocolate
- a double boiler or small saucepan
- some clean, fresh leaves (Beware of poisonous ones)
- a new paint brush

To make the leaves

1 Melt the chocolate in the double boiler.
2 Paint one side of each leaf with the chocolate. You may have to do this several times to build up a sufficient depth of chocolate.
3 When the chocolate has set, peel the leaf away and you will have some pretty chocolate leaves.

Smoke pictures

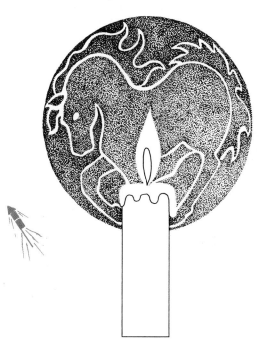

Collect together:

- a large white pottery plate
- a candle

To make the pictures

1 Light the candle and hold the plate just above the flame. Turn the plate slowly so that all of its surface gets covered with black soot.
2 Using a finger, draw pictures in the soot. Alternatively you could scratch out a picture by using a cocktail stick.
3 When you have finished with one picture hold the plate above the flame and start again.

(Young children will need to be very carefully supervised when making these pictures.)

A rocket on a stick

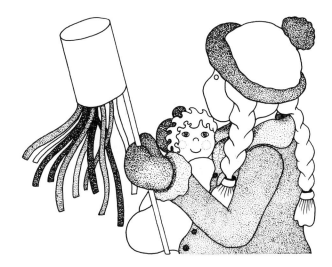

Collect together:

- 1 toilet roll tube
- 1 thin garden cane about 50cm long
- tinfoil
- old colourful magazines
- scissors
- glue and a glue brush
- Sellotape

To make the rocket

1 Cover the tube with tinfoil and sellotape this into positon.
2 Carefully sellotape one end of the garden cane inside the tube.
3 Choose some really colourful pictures from the magazines and cut these into thin strips.
4 Sellotape or glue the magazine strips so they trail from the bottom of the tube.

Do remind children that real fireworks must never be held in the hand.

Birthdays

PARTY THEMES

Making the preparations for a party may seem like hard work, but it is often half the fun for children. So allow your child to be as involved as possible. Children love to make invitations, decorations and party food, and they would also enjoy preparing some of the games listed in this section.

All the parties described here have a theme. This often makes planning the party much simpler as it provides a framework for the activities and games. Themes can be based on a colour, fairytales, a space adventure, a favourite television programme, a foreign country, a disco, or simply fancy dress. But the best source of ideas is your child. He will probably have lots of ideas of his own.

Most of the birthday cakes mentioned in this section use butter cream frosting. It is very simple for a child to make. Here is a recipe.

Butter cream frosting

- 115g butter
- 225g icing sugar
- 2 tablespoons of cold milk
- food colouring

Beat the butter until it is soft and creamy. Add the icing sugar and milk a little at a time. Finally add the food colouring.

A JUMBLE PARTY THEME

Children adore dressing up and trying on make-up. It is great fun and can lead on to more imaginative play and acting.

All you have to do is provide a very large box or boxes full of dressing-up clothes, hats, costume jewelry and shoes. A table containing some make-up, make-up removing cream, cotton wool and a few hand mirrors would also be very popular. If it is possible to arrange for a full length mirror to be available this would enable the guests to see the overall effect.

The clothes and hats needed for this party can be obtained by attending a few jumble sales before the party date. Jumble sales are marvellous places for bargains. You should be able to buy lots of colourful clothes for only a few pence, but do remember to take lots of carrier bags to the jumble sale to carry everything home in. Children find jumble sales exciting places, so don't forget to give the party girl a carrier bag and a small amount of money and ask her to hunt through the jumble with you.

If there aren't any jumble sales in your area and your own wardrobes don't provide enough old clothes, ask grandparents, aunts and friends to look out some jumble for you. Or alternatively you could ask each guest to bring an armful of clothes with them.

· To start the party, guests spend some time dressing up and applying make up. This will keep them amused for some considerable time. On the clothes theme the children might also like to design and make their own clothes. All you need to provide are some old sheets, old T-shirts, old shirts, scissors, lots of large safety pins and thick felt-tip pens. The pens can be used to draw pictures or patterns on to the fabric and the pins join the fabric together without the need for needles and cotton.

A jumble party invitation

Your child can make very colourful washing line invitation cards simply by drawing a line across

an oblong sheet of paper or card, sticking some cut out paper clothes on to the line and writing the details of the party directly on to the clothes. As you can see from the illustration, the last item on the clothes line is the "reply" slip for each guest. Obviously this mustn't be stuck down too firmly.

A jumble party cake

A Bonnet Cake

Jumble party games

A hat competition

Give the children plenty of paper streamers, crepe paper, newspaper, scissors, Sellotape, paper clips, and perhaps a stapler. Ask them to make a hat within a given time and award prizes for the most original, the prettiest and the funniest.

A shoe shop race

All the children remove their shoes. These are then placed in the centre of the room and mixed up so that the pairs are completely muddled. At a given signal the children rush to find their own shoes again and put them on. The winner is the first one with her/his own shoes on the correct feet.

Dressing the doll

Divide the children into equal teams. Provide each team with a similar box of clothes, e.g. a hat, a scarf, a dress, a pair of gloves. There should be as many articles of clothing as there are members in the team, less one.

Place the boxes at the far end of the room with each team sitting opposite their box. One member from each team acts as "doll" and goes to stand next to their clothes box. The race begins.

One at a time the team members run up to the clothes box, remove one item of clothing and put it on the "doll". The "doll" must not help in any way. The team member returns to his team and the next in line runs to the clothes box.

The winning team is the one who dresses the doll first. You could extend this game by asking the teams to dress and undress the "doll".

The Easter bonnet race

Divide the children into equal teams and ask each team to sit in a long line. Each team is given a bonnet or hat which is fastened with ribbons. The race begins.

The first member of each team puts on the bonnet and ties it under her chin. She turns to the next member of the team who unties the bow, removes the bonnet and places it on her own head, tying the bow again. The next player then removes the bonnet and so on down the line. The first team to have all tried on the bonnet wins the race.

AN ANIMAL PARTY THEME

An animal party is a real winner as animals of all kinds are very popular with children. The party decorations can of course reflect this zoo type theme. Ask each guest to bring along a home-made animal, e.g. a sock snake, or perhaps a favourite soft animal, e.g. a teddy bear. Posters of animals could be stuck on the walls of the party room or alternatively you could draw some large silhouettes of animals and use these to decorate doors, walls etc.

If your child has a favourite animal, for example horses, the posters and silhouettes could all reflect a horse theme and it might also be fun to provide each guest with a hobby horse made out of a stuffed sock pushed on to a garden cane.

An animal party invitation

Draw the face and front legs of an animal on an 8cm by 8cm piece of card. Draw the animal's tail and back legs on another 8cm by 8cm card. Stick the two pieces of card across the ends of a toilet roll rube. Wrap a piece of paper around the tube and write the party invitation on the paper.

An animal party cake

A teddy bear cake

Animal party games

Pin the tail on the donkey

This traditional game could be changed slightly. It doesn't need to be a donkey, you could have an elephant or lion. Draw a large animal minus tail on a big sheet of paper and make a mark to show where the tail should go. The children are blindfolded one at a time and asked to make a mark with a pencil or crayon where they think the tail belongs. This is a great game for "audience participation". Get them to shout out comments and instructions as the "victim" tries to work out where to put the tail. Give prizes to those children whose marks are nearest to the correct position.

Feeding time at the zoo

Sit the children in a circle and stand in the middle with a bag of sweets. Describe an animal to the children, but don't tell them what it is called. The first child to shout out the name of the animal wins a sweet. If no-one guesses, you get the sweet yourself!

Make an elephant

Each child is given a sheet of newspaper and at a given signal they must try to rip out an elephant shape. The winner is the one with the most elephant-like result. Of course it doesn't have to be an elephant, any animal could be made. If it's dark outside, why not switch out the lights and ask them to make the animal in the dark.

The alphabet zoo

Write out the letters of the alphabet, (excluding the letters ''u'' and ''x'') on some pieces of card 10cm square. Place the letters in a box or bag. Sit the children in front of you so that they can all see the letters as they are pulled one at a time out of the box. The first person to shout out the name of an animal starting with the shown letter wins the card. The overall winner is the one with the most cards at the end of the game.

A COWBOYS AND INDIANS PARTY THEME

Ask your child to help you to make some ''Wanted dead or alive'' posters to decorate the party room. These can be great fun, especially if some of the portraits and the names of the outlaws are based on the party guests.

In the summer, weather permitting, move into the garden. Here a few home-made wigwams would be greatly appreciated. To make a wigwam you simply tie 5 long, stout garden canes in a pyramid shape and drape some blankets over the canes. If you are using the garden a barbecue would of course be an excellent idea. Sausages, beefburgers and beans would complete a cowboy and Indian theme.

A cowboys and Indians party invitation

An Indian headdress makes a super invitation and the guests can of course wear it during the party. Take some long strips of card 55cm by 3cm and colour the strips with patterns, bands of colour or Indian style picture writing. On the inside of the headband write out the party invitation. Attach some real feathers or paper cut out feathers to the outside of the band. Leave the strips of card loose, so each guest can measure his own head and sellotape the band accordingly.

A cowboys and Indians party cake

A totem pole cake

Cowboys and Indians party games

Making a totem pole

Collect together lots of empty cardboard boxes, paints and glue. Cover a large area of the floor with newspaper or move out into the garden. Put aprons on the party guests and ask them to decorate and paint the boxes. When the boxes have dried sufficiently, make a totem pole by sticking them one on top of the other.

Now is the time to dance round the totem pole. Why not have some musical instruments such as bells or tambourines ready, or perhaps a tape of suitably happy music? Don't forget the cotton wool for your ears and the peace-offerings for the neighbours!

The laughing cowboy hat

The players are divided into two teams and asked to sit in two long lines opposite each other. One player stands in the middle and throws a cowboy hat up into the air. If the hat lands on the brim one team of the players must laugh, if it lands on the crown the other team must start to laugh. If any players laugh at the wrong time they are out. If any players do not laugh at all, tickle them.

War paint

Provide the children with some good quality face paints, (available from toy shops) and a few hand mirrors. Set a little competition to see who can produce the most frightening war painted face.

The Mississippi river (a game for the garden)

An area of the garden is marked out with ropes stretched out on the ground (washing lines are ideal). The area needs to be about two and a half metres wide. This is the Mississippi river. One player is chosen to be the crocodile. The cowboys and Indians must cross back and forth across the river without being caught by the crocodile. If the crocodile ticks them, they also become crocodiles and help to chase the others.

A PIRATES PARTY THEME

The decorations for this party could reflect the skull and crossbones motif. Black silhouettes of a skull and crossed bones could be painted on to posters or blown-up balloons. The treasure island map used in one of the games could also have a prominent position on one wall. Remember to stick posters up with Blu-Tack as this doesn't leave a mark.

A pirate party invitation

As you can see from the illustration the treasure island theme could easily be used for the party invitations. To make the maps look really old, an adult could slightly burn and singe the corners of each map with a burning match. They can then be rolled into tube shapes and tied with ribbon.

A pirate party cake

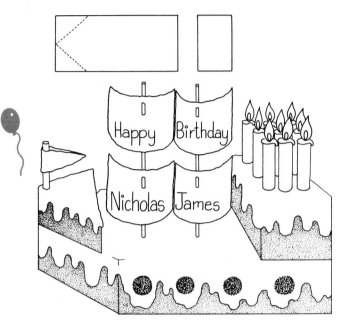

A pirate galleon

Pirate party games

Treasure Island

A large treasure island map containing such things as the "Devil's Mountain" and "Dead Man's Swamp" should be attached to the wall. On the reverse side of the map you should have made a mark to show where the treasure is buried. The children take turns at marking a spot on the map where they believe the treasure can be found. When everyone has had a turn at guessing, the real location is found and the child whose name is nearest to the mark wins the prize.

Hunt the silver coins

Before the party guests arrive cover lots and lots of chocolate buttons with tinfoil. Hide these around the room or garden and when the guests arrive, ask them to find the treasure and eat it! Metal-detectors are not normally necessary!

Treasure trove

Divide the children into two teams. At one end of the room or garden place a collection of treasures, e.g. small sweets or toys. There needs to be as many treasures as there are children in the race. On a given signal the first member of each team runs and picks up a piece of treasure and returns to the team. The next player then runs to the treasure and so on. The first team to complete the race are the winners. Of course all the players should keep their treasure.

Walk the plank

Mark out a long strip of ground by laying two washing lines opposite each other 1 metre apart. At one end of the strip place a doormat. When the music plays the children walk in a line along the centre of the strip, (i.e. the plank) around the outside of the plank and along the plank again. When the music stops the players on or nearest to the end of the plank, (i.e. the doormat) are out.

A FAIRY PARTY THEME

The first thing to do is make the party room and table look as pretty as possible. Lots of pink ribbons, tinsel, pink balloons, and silver and gold paper doilies help to create a fairy effect.

 Provide each guest with a fairy wand, i.e. a stick covered with tinfoil with either strips of tinsel or a silver star stuck on to one end. Young girls enjoy ballet dancing, especially in party frocks, and so an open space and a suitable tape of music is usually appreciated.

A fairy party invitation

This can take the form of a tinfoil or glitter covered cardboard star. Obviously one side needs to remain uncovered so that you can write out the details of the party.

A fairy party cake

A fairy

Fairy party games

Witches' hats

The players sit in a circle. Two home-made witches hats, e.g. black paper stuck into a cone shape, are passed around while the music plays. When the music stops, whoever is holding a hat must turn into a witch and must drop out of the game. The winners are the last three players who have not been turned into witches.

The goblins' cave

The players skip round in a circle to the music. A small carpet is placed in an area where the children must cross over it. This is the goblins

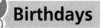
cave. When the music stops, any child standing in the cave must drop out of the game. If there is no one standing in the cave, the player nearest to the cave is out. The winners are the last three children not captured by the goblin.

Magic spells

The players sit in a large circle. One player stands in the middle of the circle and is blindfolded. She is given a magic wand, i.e. a rolled up tube of newspaper covered in tinfoil. She is turned three or four times and then tries to find her way towards someone in the circle. She then gently taps the person three times with her magic wand and says "Magic spells" each time. The touched player must repeat the words "Magic spells" and the blindfolded fairy must try to guess who is speaking. If she can guess correctly, the players exchange places. If the fairy guesses incorrectly, she must try again at least once before another player has a turn.

A NEWSPAPER PARTY THEME

The decorations for this party couldn't be less expensive. Old clean newspapers can be used in a variety of ways. The party table itself could be covered with it. Newspaper could be turned into garlands by cutting it into strips and threading the strips through each other to make a newspaper chain. All prizes and going home presents could be wrapped in it. And if you feel like serving a traditional dish, fish and chips always taste better out of newspaper.

A newspaper party invitation

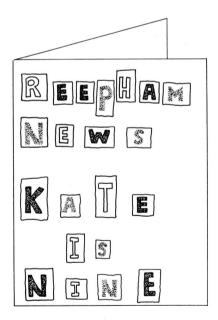

These can be simply made by cutting out the individual letters for all the words on the invitations from old newspaper headlines. Stick the letters together in the correct order on to a sheet of plain white paper.

Alternatively, fold a piece of cardboard in half, cover the outside with newspaper and write the details of the party inside rather like a news item, e.g.

"Stop Press News! Nicholas James is having a Newspaper party!"

A newspaper party cake

Make a rectangular cake and cover it with white icing. The wording on the cake could be written in a typical newspaper headline style, e.g. "Express news. Sophie Eloise is ten today." Surround the cake with a folded newspaper strip which has had a frill cut along one edge.

Newspaper party games

Newspaper parcels

Give each child an individual, well-wrapped parcel of the sort used in pass-the-parcel. At a given signal the players must unwrap the layers of newspaper in order to discover the secret in the middle, i.e. a small bar of chocolate. The winner is the first one to reach the centre of his parcel.

Advertisements

Make a list of some well known advertisement headlines. Write these out on individual sheets of paper but leave out the name of the product which is being advertised, e.g. "a – – – – a day helps you work, rest, and play." Give each child a list and a pencil and ask them to fill in the missing words.

Railway carriages

A few weeks before the party, obtain a selection of national and local newspapers from different days of the week. You will need one for each guest. Take the newspapers apart and put them back together again with all the pages muddled up and different newspapers mixed together.

During the party, arrange the chairs to look like the inside of a railway carriage. Ask the children to sit on the chairs. Give each guest a muddled up newspaper and at a given signal, ask the guests to find their "complete" paper. Lots of noisy chaos should follow!

Newspaper hats or doilies

Give the children lots of newspaper, scissors, paperclips and Sellotape.

Ask them to make a hat. The winner is the one who creates the most original design.

Alternatively the children could be asked to make a doily by folding the newspaper several times to make a small square and cutting out shapes from the outside edge of the square. When the newspaper is opened out it looks very pretty.

The agony column

Give each child a pencil and paper and divide the guests into two teams. The children in one team secretly write letters to the agony aunt with the silliest problems they can think of, e.g. "My cat has grown an extra tail and sings the national anthem in the bath."

The other team members secretly write out silly replies, e.g. "I suggest you place a bowl of jelly on your head and sleep with your feet pointing south."

When everyone has finished you pick out and read pairs of questions and answers. If you get the feeling this is how certain well-known columnists make their living, you may be not too far wrong!

Fan the newspaper kipper

Before the party cut out some large fish shapes from single sheets of newspaper, one fish per child. Ask the children to stand in a line and place a newspaper fish on the floor in front of each of them. Give each child a folded newspaper and ask them to fan the kippers across the room. They mustn't actually touch the fish. The winner is the first one to reach the finishing line.

BIRTHDAY SURPRISES

Biscuit faces

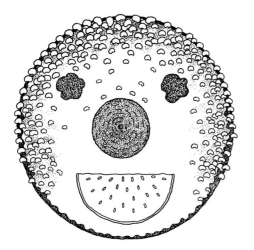

Collect together:

- a bowl for mixing
- a knife for spreading
- round plain biscuits, for example digestives
- 6 tablespoons of cream cheese
- 6 tablespoons of soft margarine
- raisins
- thin slices of carrot
- thin slices of cucumber cut in half
- cress

To make the faces

1 Cream together the cream cheese and margarine.
2 Spread the cheese mixture on to the biscuits. Be sure to spead the mixture to the edge of the biscuit.
3 Arrange the fruit and vegetables to form a face.

Popcorn

Collect together:

- 8 tablespoons of oil
- 125g popcorn kernels
- 4 tablespoons of clear honey
- semicircles of paper 33cm wide (one for each guest)
- Sellotape
- a saucepan with a tight fitting lid
- a large bowl
- a wooden spoon

To make the popcorn

1 Heat the oil in the saucepan over a high heat.
2 Add a quarter of the corn. Put the lid back on the pan and shake the pan constantly. Wait until the popping stops, which is usually only a couple of minutes.
3 Remove the pan from the heat. Pour 1 tablespoon of the honey over the popcorn and stir well. Put the popcorn into a bowl and repeat the process with the rest of the popcorn.

To make the cones for the popcorn

Fold a semicircle of paper into a cone shape and sellotape it into position.

Party guests love to go home with a cone of popcorn.

Kitten cakes

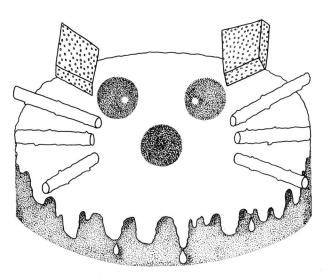

Collect together:

- a large mixing bowl
- a blunt knife
- a wooden spoon
- a swiss roll
- Smarties
- jelly diamonds
- chocolate sticks
- 225g icing sugar
- 100g soft margarine
- 1 tablespoon of cocoa powder
- 2 tablespoons of milk

To make the cakes

1 Mix together the icing sugar, soft margarine, cocoa powder and milk in the large bowl. The result should resemble thick chocolate cream.
2 Cut the swiss roll into slices.
3 Use the knife to thickly spread the chocolate cream on to the slices of swiss roll.

4 Create a kitten's face on each slice of cake by using:
jelly diamonds for ears,
Smarties for the eyes and nose,
chocolate sticks for the whiskers.

These little cakes are easy for children to prepare before the party starts.

Individual candle cakes

Collect together:

- a small iced cake for each party guest
- a birthday candle for each cake

All children love to blow candles out, so why not provide each guest with an individual birthday cake, i.e. a small cake with a candle stuck in it. Then when the birthday boy or girl blows out their candles, the guests can join in the fun. And when the room is full of lighted candles, it looks extremely pretty.

An edible zoo

Collect together:

- cocktail sticks
- chunks of fresh fruit or raw vegetables
- chunks of cold cooked sausage and cheese

If you provide the party guests with the ingredients they can prepare their own party food. Children can arrange the food on the cocktail sticks to create monsters, pets, or wild animals. Then they can eat them!

A birthday balloon card

Collect together:

- a piece of thick card 40cm by 24cm
- a felt-tip pen
- crayons
- scissors
- a balloon

To make the card

1 Fold the card in half so that the front of the card measures 20cm by 24cm. Write a birthday message inside the card.

2 Draw and colour a large happy clown's face on the front of the card.
3 Using the scissors, make a small hole in one corner of the clown's mouth.
4 The balloon can now be blown up (not too fully); and the knotted end inserted through the hole. Of course the card can be sent with the balloon deflated and merely threaded through the hole. Then the recipient can blow the balloon up for herself.

A birthday badge

Collect together:

- a circle of card. You can easily make this by drawing round a small coffee cup on to a sheet of card and then cutting it out.
- crayons
- scissors
- Sellotape
- a large safety pin

To make the badge

1 Draw the birthday number on to the front of the card and decorate the number with patterns or pictures. If the birthday child has a special interest, e.g. football, the pictures on the badge could reflect this theme.
2 Attach the safety pin to the back of the card with a strip of Sellotape.